The Adventures of Aspen the Bee

Story: Priya Sekhri & Katherine Su
Illustrations: Katherine Su

Includes fun facts!

In a hive so cozy, snug, and neat,
Lived Aspen the bee, with tiny feet.
She buzzed and hummed from cell to cell,
But deep in her heart, she didn't feel well.

"I'm just so bored," she'd quietly sigh,
"Make honey? Guard wax? Just buzz and fly?"
While others danced to share where they'd been,
Aspen dreamed of a world beyond the queen.

"I don't want nectar, not pollen or wax.
I want new places and different tracks."
So one warm morning, just after dawn,
She zipped past the hive—and soon was gone.

Down to the forest, where shadows swayed,
She found her friend Ant, in a leafy parade.
"Why do you march in this perfect line?"
Aspen asked, as her wings caught sunshine.

"We follow trails of scent," Ant said.
"They lead to crumbs, to seeds, to bread.
But it's your flowers that give us cheer—
Without pollinators, they'd disappear!"

Ants can navigate well through paths even in areas with little light, like underground, because of little scent dots called "pheromones"! These pheromone trails are like little dots and they disappear quickly within a few minutes.

Be careful and follow close so you don't get lost!

There's a subfamily of termites with a green thumb! They like to grow gardens with a special type of fungus called Termitomyces mushrooms. These mushrooms then grow special structures (combs) that the termites love to eat!

Next she saw Termite, chewing through wood.
"You live underground?" "Yes—home is good!
I farm fungi with careful care,
But need fallen leaves and blooms in the air.

You bees spread seeds and grow the trees—
So even I depend on bees!"

Scopas!

Honeybees use pollen baskets (scopas) on their hind legs to carry pollen from plant to plant. This helps plants get pollinated (this is how flowers make seeds), so more plants can grow!

Aspen blinked. "I never knew…
My sisters help the forest too?"

Up in the sky, where the cattails swayed,
She found Dragonfly in a quick cascade.
"I chase mosquitoes, I skim the streams,
But flowers support the food of dreams.

Without bees helping plants to thrive,
The web of life just can't survive!"

Dragonflies are master hunters! Their wings made of reinforced chitin make them one of the best fliers in the insect world and their compound eyes have ultra light-sensitive proteins (opsins), allowing them to see with great precision even in the slightest degree of light!

ZIP

Through a cave where the glowworms glowed,
Aspen drifted, her wonder showed.
Webs like lace, all sticky-bright,
Caught tiny bugs in shimmering light.

Native to the caves of New Zealand, glowworms are the larvae of a type of flying gnat – not worms at all! These glowing babies with bright, bioluminescent abdomens light up cave ceilings with sticky, silk threads spun from their spit. The threads reflect their glow and help attract and reel in prey for dinner!

Glowworm winked from her silken thread,
"Flowers feed flies who feed me instead.
Your kind starts it all—with each petal you kiss.
Bees may be small, but nothing's like this."

Aspen sat still, in quiet delight—
The stars of the forest lit up the night.
"I thought my hive life was boring and plain,
But now I see—I must train again!"

Just then a call rang loud and true,
"Aspen! Where are you? We need you!"
A worker bee's voice, familiar and dear,
Brought her back home with wings in high gear.

Back at the hive, she trained with pride,
Flying to flowers with pollen to guide.
From lavender fields to orchards sweet,
She danced the dance on six tiny feet.

So if you see a bee zipping by,
  Whisper a thanks as she paints the sky.

For like Aspen, she's brave, and wise from afar—
A pollinator, nature's bright shining star.

The End!

A Message From the Authors!

Aspen the bee might live in a magical forest, but real bees like her are facing big problems in the real world. Honeybees are disappearing, and fast. Scientists call this *colony collapse disorder*. But why is it happening?

Climate Change: Bees need flowers, and flowers need the right weather. But as the planet gets hotter, flowers bloom too early—or not at all! Without food from flowers, bees go hungry.

Deforestation: When forests are cut down or cities grow too big, bees lose their homes. No trees means no wildflowers, which means no bees.

Pesticides and Pollution: Some chemicals sprayed on plants to keep bugs away are also harmful to bees. They get sick or forget how to find their way back to the hive.

Why Should We Care?: Bees aren't just cute and buzzy—they help make one out of every three bites of food we eat! Apples, strawberries, almonds, even chocolate all need bees to grow. Without bees, the world would lose color, flavor, and life.

So, what can you do to help bees like Aspen thrive?

Plant Bee-Friendly Flowers: Choose blooms like lavender, daisies, or sunflowers in your yard, garden, or even a flowerpot!

Say No to Spray: Ask grown-ups to avoid using bug sprays and weed killers where bees might land, as the chemicals have the potential to make the bees sick.

Give Bees a Drink: Leave out a shallow dish with pebbles and water. Bees get thirsty too!

Spread the Buzz: Tell your friends, your teacher, or your class about what you've learned from this book. Even small voices can make a big buzz.

If you'd like to learn more about the bee crisis or donate to an organization fighting for our bees, flip the page to learn more about the organization joining us in our fight for honeybee survival.

And remember, Just like Aspen, YOU can be a hero for the hive. Even the smallest actions help keep nature buzzing and blooming!

Bee kind. Bee curious. Bee the change.

Lots of love,
Priya and Katherine

Pollinator Partnership:

The Pollinator Partnership is an incredible organization that helps bees like Aspen thrive through their conservation-based advocacy and their incredible dedication to education. They teach farmers, gardeners, and even kids like yourself how to plant pollinator-friendly gardens full of colorful blooms. They also help protect natural habitats where wild pollinators live and make sure that people understand how important these creatures are for our planet. From creating fun learning materials to organizing big events like Pollinator Week, they bring people together to celebrate and care for our buzzing friends. Thanks to the Pollinator Partnership, more flowers are blooming, more crops are growing, and more pollinators are safe and happy. They believe that even the smallest hands can make a big difference—and so do we!

If you'd like to get involved, visit their page at www.pollinator.org or scan the QR code below.

Protect their lives. Preserve ours.